Children of the World

My Life in
KENYA

Alex Woolf

Cavendish
Square

New York

Published in 2015 by Cavendish Square Publishing, LLC
243 5th Avenue, Suite 136, New York, NY 10016

Copyright © Arcturus Holdings Limited

First Edition

Website: cavendishsq.com

This publication represents the opinions and views of the author based on his or her
personal experience, knowledge, and research. The information in this book serves
as a general guide only. The author and publisher have used their best efforts in
preparing this book and disclaim liability rising directly or indirectly from the use and
application of this book.

CPSIA Compliance Information: Batch #WW15CSQ

All websites were available and accurate when this book was sent to press.

Library of Congress Cataloging-in-Publication Data

Woolf, Alex, 1964- author.
 My life in Kenya / Alex Woolf.
     pages cm. — (Children of the world)
 ISBN 978-1-50260-045-5 (hardcover) ISBN 978-1-50260-055-4 (paperback)
 ISBN 978-1-50260-057-8 (ebook)
1. Kenya—Juvenile literature. 2. Children—Kenya—Juvenile literature. I. Title. II.
Series: Children of the world (New York, N.Y.)

 DT433.522.W66 2015
 967.62—dc23

2014026349

Editor: Joe Harris
Designer: Ian Winton

All photography courtesy of Boniface Muthoni / Demotix / Corbis

Contents

Getting Up

5:45 AM

Hi! I'm Esther. I am ten years old and I live with my mother, father, and sister here in Nairobi, Kenya.

Esther says...
Each weekday morning, when I wake up, I put on my school uniform.

Our house has two rooms. I share one room with my sister, Grace. My parents sleep in the other room.

I wake up at 5:45 AM. Sometimes I find it hard to get up so early, especially between June and September when the mornings are colder.

I use the outside tap to wash my face.

My Country

Kenya is a **country** in East Africa. It lies on the **equator**, so it has a hot **climate**. Nairobi is the **capital city**.

Breakfast

Mom makes us breakfast. This morning she makes us an omelette and **chai**, which is a spiced tea from India.

Esther says...

I love the smell of chai. It wakes me up!

Sometimes Mom makes us a thin porridge from **cornmeal**, called *uji* (OO-jee). But my favorite breakfast food is *mandazi* (muhn-DAH-zee), a sweet, flat doughnut.

6

Mandazi is fried bread made with coconut milk. My mother gets up early to make it and we eat it warm for breakfast, or cold later in the day.

After breakfast, Grace and I brush our teeth in the yard.

Chai

This is a very popular drink in Kenya. The tea, milk, and sugar are put into cold water and then brought to a boil.

Walking to School

6:30 AM

At 6:30, I must leave to go to school. I say goodbye to my family. It takes me twenty minutes to walk to school.

Esther says...

Bye-bye Grace. Soon you'll be old enough to go to school, too!

Nairobi is a huge city with more than 3 million people. I live in a small part of it called Westlands.

I walk some of the way to school with my friend Linda.

On the way to school, I stop to buy a snack.

Money

The **currency** of Kenya is the Kenyan shilling (Ksh). Sometimes Mom gives me 50 Ksh, which is enough to buy a drink and a bag of chips.

Lesson Time

The school bell rings at 7:00 AM. During class, **I** sit next to my deskmate, Anne. Everybody speaks English at school.

Esther says ...

When I grow up, I would like to be a school teacher.

This school is called Nairobi County Primary. Our lessons include Christian Religion Education (CRE), Mathematics, English, **Swahili**, and Social Studies.

I think I am lucky to study here. There are about fifty people in my class. However, some schools in Kenya have up to two hundred students in each class.

We have to work quietly during lesson time.

Going to School

In Kenya, the law says that all children must go to school. Most children attend school from the age of six or seven.

Playtime

10:00 AM

At ten o'clock, we have our morning break. After three hours in a classroom, it feels good to get out in the fresh air.

Esther says ...

I bet you can't catch me!

We are lucky to have so much space to run around. Sometimes we play soccer, which we call football, or have running and jumping competitions.

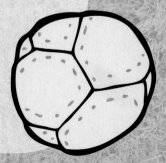

We like to play a game called Kati. It's a lot like **dodgeball**. Each team throws balls at the other. If you're hit with a ball, you are out.

We are playing tug-of-war, but we don't have a rope!

Green City

People call Nairobi "the green city in the sun" because it has so many parks and gardens. My favorite is Uhuru Park. I go there sometimes on weekends.

In the Library

We have been given permission to visit the school library.
It has books in English and Swahili.

Esther says ...
I love books about animals. So does my friend Damaris!

The Lonely Giraffe
by Peter Blight

9 Glory Monday

There are many languages spoken in Kenya, but the two main ones are English and Swahili. I speak English at school and Swahili at home.

We are lucky. Very few schools in Kenya have their own library. My favorite book in the library is *Gamba the Gecko*, about a **gecko** who wants to play the drums.

There are places in the library where we can sit and read.

We Love Books

Books are very important to us in Kenya, because most people in the country have no access to the **Internet**.

Eating Lunch

1:00 PM

It is time for lunch. We go to the dining hall, pick up our plates, and join the line to be served.

Esther says ...
After such a busy morning, I'm feeling very hungry!

For lunch today we are having stew. This is a typical dish of Kenya: chunks of meat, potatoes, and carrots, served with rice.

16

Another popular dish in our country is *ugali (oo-GAH-lee)*. This is a thick paste made from cornmeal **starch** and it tastes great with fried vegetables or meat stew.

It is the custom in our country to always eat with your right hand.

Hands are okay!

Some students bring spoons from home. The rest of us use our hands. We always wash our hands before and after a meal.

Afternoon Lessons

In the afternoon, we have art, which is my favorite subject, and mathematics, which isn't! I like our teacher, but she can be quite strict.

Esther says ...

Jamila and I can't wait for our art class to start.

There is a big **shortage** of teachers in our country. The average school has just four teachers. I want to be a teacher.

Today, I am practicing drawing simple objects like houses, trees, and bottles.

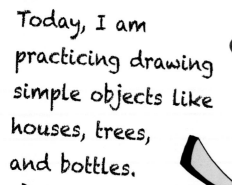

I am waiting to hand in my math worksheet. I hope I get a good grade!

School Year

Our school year runs from January to November. We have vacations in April, August, and December.

Walking Home

School ends at four o'clock. Everybody is in a rush to leave. Some students are picked up by their parents, but I must walk home.

Esther says ...

I enjoyed school today. But I know I must study hard to achieve my dream.

To become a teacher, I must go to secondary school and then to teacher training college. The nearest secondary school is too far to walk to, so I'll have to **board**.

I'm feeling hungry, so I eat my chips.

Home again! I change out of my uniform.

The Cost of School

My parents must pay for my room and **board** and my uniform if **I** go to secondary school. This will be expensive, so they are saving up for it.

Fetching Water

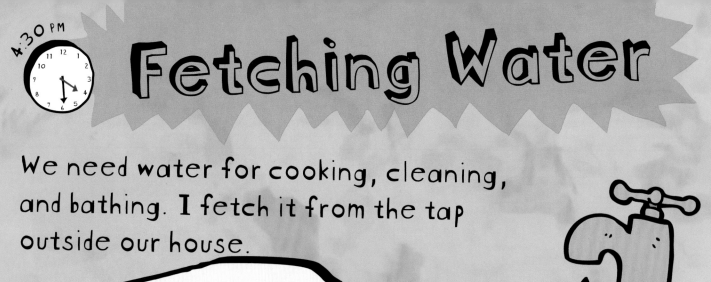

We need water for cooking, cleaning, and bathing. I fetch it from the tap outside our house.

Esther says ...

This will be for tomorrow's chai.

We are lucky to have clean water so close. I have heard that 17.5 million people in this country are not able to use safe water in their daily lives.

In some parts of rural Kenya, people have to travel long distances to fetch water from a well. Even here in Nairobi, women can spend over two hours a day fetching water.

We will use this for washing up and cleaning the floor.

Sanitation

We don't have our own toilet. Most people don't in Kenya. We share a **latrine** with our neighbors.

At the Market

Mom needs to buy some fresh groceries for the evening meal, so we walk to the market. Everything looks so delicious!

Esther says ...
I love visiting the market. It's very loud, but people are so friendly.

In the market, prices are not fixed. The stand holders expect everyone to bargain. We must try to persuade them to give us a good price!

We buy carrots, tomatoes, peppers, and **yams**. Mom asks me to choose the ripest vegetables. We are having stew again tonight, but I don't mind!

This stand is selling bags of root vegetables. I try to choose the best one!

Kenyan Markets

You can buy all sorts of things at outdoor markets, not just food. Sometimes you can find beautiful art and crafts.

Evening Meal

It is time to prepare dinner. I help Mom by chopping the vegetables. She then boils them in a saucepan on the stove.

Esther says...

This tomato will taste good in the stew!

Mom cooks on a gas stove. A man comes once a month and refills the cylinder with **cooking gas**.

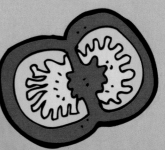

We must buy fresh food every day, because we don't have a refrigerator to store it. Tonight, the meat in our stew is goat. Sometimes we have chicken.

Chapatis

Chapatis (Ka-PA-tis) are popular in Kenya. The dough is rolled out and fried in oil so they're crispy on the outside and gooey on the inside. They taste great with stew.

Going to Bed

After dinner, we wash up and then clean the outside area. We must be quick, because the sun is setting. Soon it will be too dark to see.

Esther says ...

It would be easier to do these dishes if the water was hot.

Winnie lives next door. Her family shares the outside area with us. She is my age. I enjoy chatting with her as we work.

It's already getting dark as Grace, Winnie and I clean the outside area.

It's been a long day. At last I can snuggle down on my sofa. Good night!

Electricity

Today, 60 percent of Nairobians lack electricity. One day **I** hope we'll be able to light our homes. A company is aiming to turn waste into fuel to bring power to people like us.

Glossary

board (*noun*) The providing of regular meals when you stay somewhere.

board (*verb*) Receive regular meals when you stay somewhere.

capital city The city in a country where the government is located.

chai A type of Indian tea, usually made by boiling the tea leaves with milk, sugar and spices such as cardamom.

chapati A type of thin Indian pancake.

climate The weather conditions found in a particular place over a long period of time.

cooking gas A flammable gas used as a fuel in cookers.

cornmeal The edible part of corn ground to powder.

currency The money used in a particular country.

dodgeball A sport in which players in a circle try to hit opponents inside the circle with an inflated ball, forcing them out of the game.

equator An imaginary line drawn around Earth, which is equally distant from both poles.

gecko A type of lizard that is common in warm regions.

Internet The global computer network.

latrine An outdoor toilet, usually set up over a pit dug in the ground.

sanitation The conditions of public health, especially access to clean drinking water and adequate disposal of human waste.

shortage A situation where there is not enough of something.

starch A substance found in cereals and potatoes that is an important part of the human diet.

Swahili A language widely spoken in East Africa. It is one of the official languages of Kenya, and is also known as Kiswahili.

yam The edible tuber (underground stem) of a climbing plant commonly found in warm countries.

Further Information

Websites

www.kids-4-kenya.org/learn-about-kenya
A general introduction to Kenya with sections on history, religion, language, schools, and other topics.

www.our-africa.org/kenya
All about Kenya, its people, food, daily life, culture, wildlife, and many other topics.

www.teachingdrums.com/Kenya.htm
A single-page profile of Kenya, with useful links to other sites.

www.3dgeography.co.uk/#!facts-about-kenya/c14vh
Lists of interesting facts about Kenya, its geography, people, transport, and animals.

www.timeforkids.com/destination/kenya
Facts about Kenya, including a sightseeing guide, Swahili phrases, and a day in the life of a typical Kenyan child.

Further Reading

Bojang, Alison Brownlie. *Kenya*. Countries in Our World. London, England: Franklin Watts, 2013.

Bowden, Rob. *Kenya*. The Changing Faces Of. London, England: Wayland, 2007.

Dahl, Michael. *Kenya*. Countries of the World. Chicago, IL: Capstone Press, 2009.

Farrell, Tish. *Kenya*. Changing World. London, England: Arcturus Publishing, 2010.

Harrison, Paul. *Kenya*. Discover Countries. London, England: Wayland, 2010.

Williams, Karen Lynn, and Wendy Stone. *Beatrice's Dream: Life in an African Slum*. London, England: Frances Lincoln, 2013.

Index